D1217222

OUR NEW YORK

SEPT 11TH - OCT 28TH 2001

FROM TOMMY HILFIGER PHOTOGRAPHED BY ANNE MENKE

September 11, 2001 was a regular morning in New York, not unlike the countless beautiful mornings I have enjoyed here over the years. But that day would change our lives and New York forever...

That morning I found myself wandering the streets in a state of disbelief, shock, anger and bewilderment after I fled my loft downtown, four blocks away from the World Trade Center, and ran with no idea where to go. The things I saw and experienced that day defy all words and imagination. As reality started to sink in, the unity and love of everyone I encountered in the streets poured out. Everywhere, I saw couples holding hands, people hugging and strangers helping. It was then that I truly started to understand what the flag stands for and what it means to those who live here. Not able to return home, and having with me only a Polaroid camera, I started taking pictures of the way the city and its people expressed themselves.

As the days passed, I noticed that the feeling of unity and defiance grew stronger and stronger, as people chose to unite and stand together, irrespective of their race or religion. I am not an American but I am inspired by this great city and its wonderful people. I wanted to express my feelings of just how great a city and a country this is; I felt the best way to do so was through these images. Patriotism is a way of life, and I am proud and lucky to live in this great country.

I LOVE NY

A. Menke

Anne Menke

The tragic events of September 11, 2001 left me, like millions of Americans, forever changed.

I watched in disbelief as the World Trade Center towers crumbled to the ground, taking with them thousands of lives. At that moment, I realized life would never be the same for us as New Yorkers, Americans and human beings. Everything was different, except the steadfast beacon of hope uniting us as Americans. The flag.

A few weeks later, Sgt. Jerry Kane from the New York City Police Department escorted me through Ground Zero, an experience so profound and painful it left me speechless. On our way, I was inspired by the flags that hung in every imaginable corner of the city. I have always loved our flag and all that it represents, but that day I truly felt its unifying force. The Stars and Stripes emerged undaunted as an enduring symbol of freedom, strength, diversity and compassion.

Overcome with patriotism and pride, the idea for this book was born. Coincidentally the next day, my dear friend Anne Menke showed me the incredible photos she captured of the flag in the wake of this tragedy. Together we created this book, agreeing that proceeds should benefit the Twin Towers Fund, with monies going directly to victims' families. In that same spirit, it was an honor for our company to donate thousands of much needed flags to the Mayor's office and over $1 million in aid to the relief efforts.

This book is dedicated to the heroes of September 11: The courageous firefighters, policemen and women and emergency professionals. The endless stream of volunteers. The families and friends of the victims. The people of New York City. Mayor Rudolph Giuliani, who showed us that leadership, is more than command.

There are no words to describe my feelings about the unwavering American spirit. Only photos.

Tommy Hilfiger

Tommy Hilfiger

George Washington Bridge, September 20th, 2001

Chambers and Church, October 2nd, 2001

Houston Street, September 21st, 2001

Canal Street, September 20th, 2001

Ground Zero, October 26th, 2001

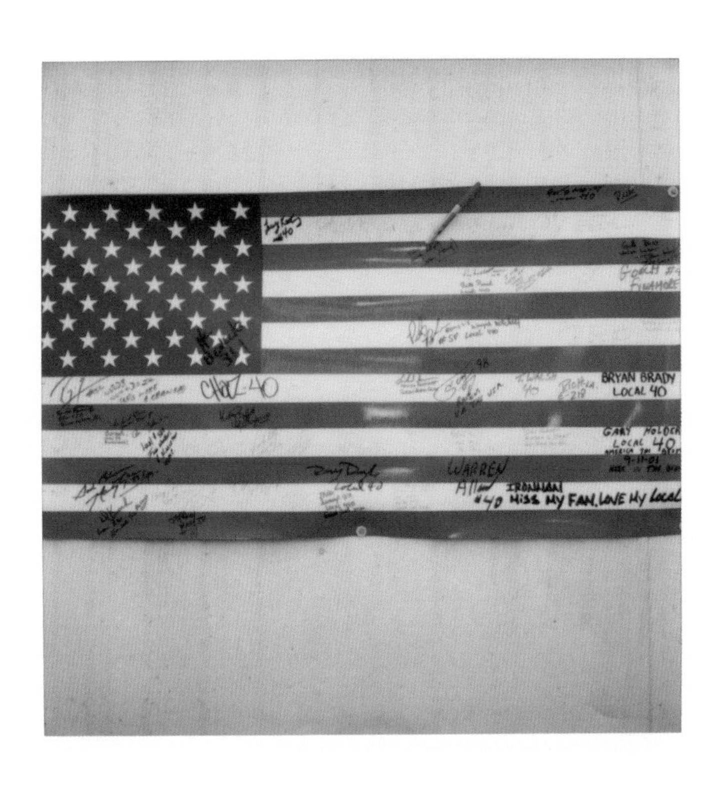

Ground Zero, October 26th, 2001

Varick Street, October 2nd, 2001

North Moore Street, October 17th, 2001

Engine 24, September 20th, 2001

Engine 14, September 14th, 2001

West Village, October 13th, 2001

Varick Street, September 13th, 2001

West 14th Street, September 22nd, 2001

View from 21st Street, October 1st, 2001

Canal Street, September 23rd, 2001

Church Street, September 17th, 2001

Noho, September 26th, 2001

East 3rd Street, September 13th, 2001

East 3rd Street, September 12th, 2001

West Broadway, September 18th, 2001

Patrol 2, September 24th, 2001

Patrol 2, September 20th, 2001

West 4th Street, October 16th, 2001

Beekman Street, September 29th, 2001

Chambers Street, September 26th, 2001

Stock Exchange, October 10th, 2001

East Village, September 17th, 2001

Engine 24, September 18th, 2001

Fifth Avenue, September 25th, 2001

Veteran Flag on Broome Street, September 17th, 2001

Cab Driver, October 18th, 2001

Engine 24, September 21st, 2001

Ground Zero, October 26th, 2001

Avenue of the Americas, September 17th, 2001

Canal Street, October 11th, 2001

Volunteer Workers, October 19th, 2001

Engine 140, October 27th, 2001

Ground Zero, October 26th, 2001

Broadway, October 17th, 2001

Ground Zero, October 26th, 2001

Ladder 8, October 26th, 2001

Ground Zero, October 26th, 2001

Soho, September 30th, 2001

Greenwich Street, October 13th, 2001

New Jersey, September 16th, 2001

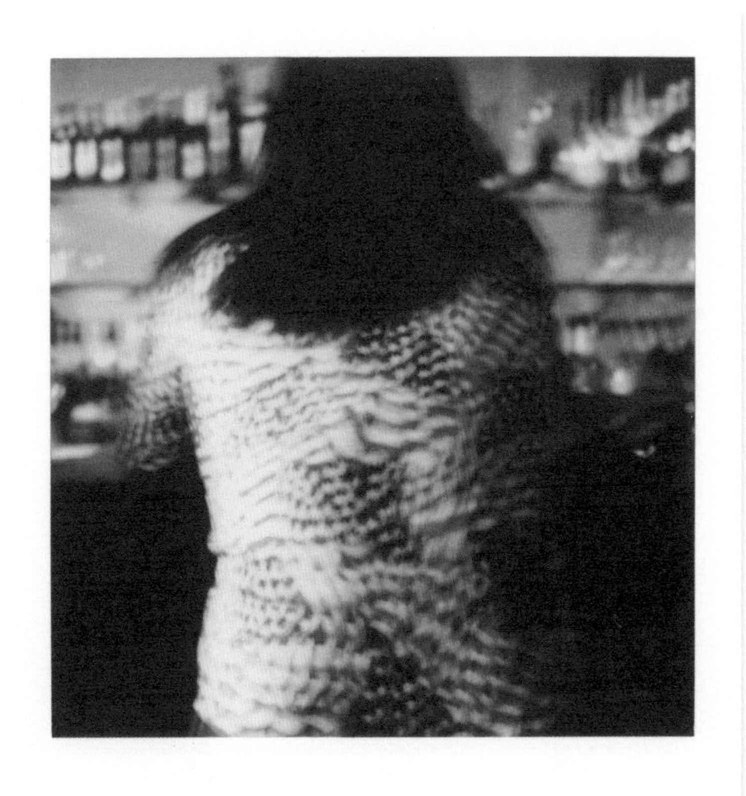

Noodle Shop, September 21st, 2001

Walker Street, September 18th, 2001

Ground Zero, October 26th, 2001

Washington Market Park, September 30th, 2001

34th Street, October 18th, 2001

Engine 7, October 11th, 2001

Varick Street, October 26th, 2001

Chinatown, October 11th, 2001

Soho, September 20th, 2001

Central Post Office, September 24th, 2001

Post Office, September 25th, 2001

Fifth Avenue, September 25th, 2001

Eighth Avenue, September 19th, 2001

Long Island, September 19th, 2001

Greek Restaurant Downtown, September 29th, 2001

West Broadway, September 29th, 2001

Madison Square Park, September 18th, 2001

Soho, September 30th, 2001

West Broadway, September 13th, 2001

Union Square, September 21st, 2001

Fifth Avenue, September 24th, 2001

Christopher Street, September 15th, 2001

East Village, September 17th, 2001

Ground Zero, October 26th, 2001

Chambers Street, October 15th, 2001

West 39th Street, September 29th, 2001

Engine 140 at Ladder 8, October 26th, 2001

Erickson Place, October 17th, 2001

Ground Zero, October 26th, 2001

Downtown, September 14th, 2001

Fifth Avenue, September 25th, 2001

Chocolate Shop, October 1st, 2001

Ground Zero, October 26th, 2001

West Street, September 29th, 2001

Engine 10, October 26th, 2001

Union Square, September 21st, 2001

Times Square, October 9th, 2001

Chambers Street, September 29th, 2001

Coffee Shop, September 21st, 2001

West Houston Street, September 17th, 2001

West 14th Street, September 21st, 2001

After Memorial, October 28th, 2001

Ground Zero, October 26th, 2001

Duane Street, October 26th, 2001

Ground Zero, October 26th, 2001

Ground Zero, October 26th, 2001

Varick Street, October 18th, 2001

Church Street after Memorial, October 28th 2001

Wall Street, October 16th, 2001

Greenwich Street, September 30th, 2001

Engine 6, October 14th, 2001

Ground Zero, October 26th, 2001

Engine 10, October 26th, 2001

East 3rd Street, September 12th, 2001

School Kids PS 234, October 16th, 2001

Ground Zero, October 26th, 2001

Church Street, September 17th, 2001

Engine 14, September 14th, 2001

New Jersey, September 15th, 2001

Washington Square, September 17th, 2001

Ground Zero, October 26th, 2001

Christopher Street, September 13th, 2001

Union Square, September 14th, 2001

Our sincerest thanks to the following people and companies for donating their time, services and efforts in producing this project. Without their generosity, this tribute and the subsequent donations to the Twin Towers Fund would not have been possible.

A.Marcus Group
Avery Baker
Caren Bell
Clear Channel Media
Color Edge
Domtar, Inc
Peter Connolly
Mollena Fabricant, Office of the Mayor
Dustin Horowitz
Carolyn Iglesias
Sergeant Jerry Kane, NYPD
Lauren Kourakos
Larry Levy, Office of the Mayor
Lloyd (+co)
MPL Productions
PMI Management
Carrie Bartlett Schwartz
Signmasters
Ticketmaster
Guy Vickers
Bridget Wilson

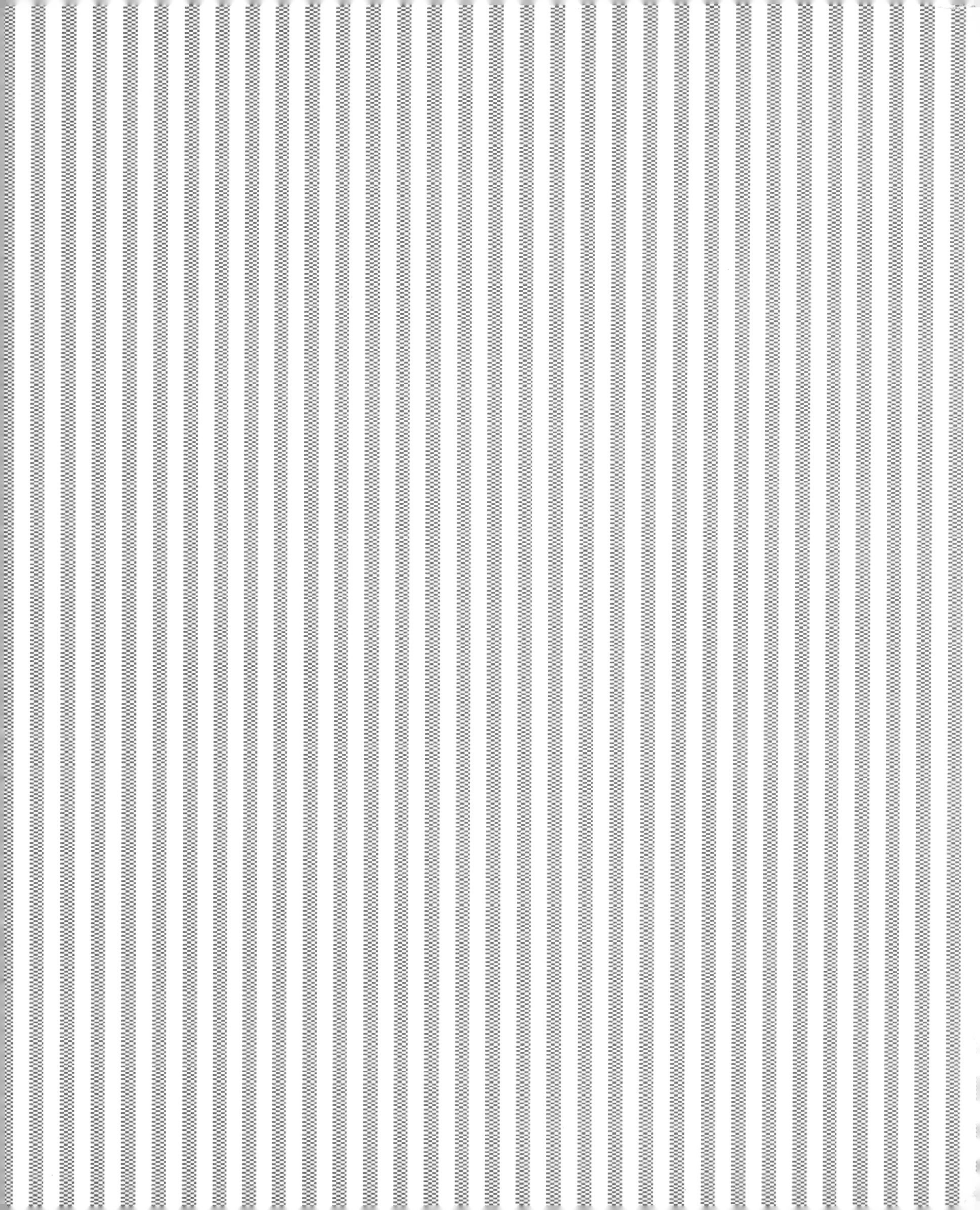